Scripture Memorization Made Possible:

Moving Beyond Rote to Memorize
Large Portions of the Bible

Melissa B/Leilani Charis

Copyright © 2014 Leilani Charis
Scripture taken from the HOLY BIBLE, NEW INTERNATIONAL VERSION ®. COPYRIGHT © 1973, 1978, 1984 by International Bible Society. Used by permission of Zondervan. All rights reserved.

Cover Design: Leilani Charis
Cover Images: © Scanrail/Big Stock Photo, Inc, ©Rich Carey/BigStock Photo, ©Fredleonero/BigStock Photo, ©Slidezero/BigStock Photo, © vkara/Fotolia, Inc
All rights reserved.

ISBN 10-1500750433

ISBN-13: 978—1500750435

ACKNOWLEDGMENTS

Mom, Gary, Jon, Paul, Bruce, Dawn, Terry, Cyndi, Scott, Lalena, Jordan, Fritz, Sharon, Melissa and the CTCI kids, Grace and so many others who have read, tested, corrected, supported and encouraged. There is nothing more beautiful than His church.

CONTENTS

1 The Bible in the Blackness 7
2 The Power of the Word 9
3 A Journey in Memorization 12
4 Walking with the Holy Spirit 16
5 The Filmmaking Memorization Process 19
6 Step One: Research the Relationships 22
7 Step Two: See the Movie 27
8 Hide and Seek 31
10 Step Three: Tell the Story 39
11 Step Four: Attach the Words 41
12 Out Loud 43
13 Step Five: Give it Away 45
14 Forget It! 48
15 Memorizing Lists 50
16 How to Get Started 55
17 Caution Lights 57
18 Maximizing Memory 59
19 A Woman at War 61

DEDICATION

To Jesus. Who fulfilled everything for us so that we might be fully filled with Him

"Your Words were found and I ate them, and your words became to me a joy and the delight of my heart, for I am called by your name, O Lord, God of hosts."

Jeremiah 15:16, ESV

1 The Bible in the Blackness

It was the unthinkable. Howard Rutledge was flying his fighter plane in the middle of a heated dogfight when his plane suddenly exploded. Wrestling with the controls he found himself plummeting to the earth. Frantically he reached for the cord to eject but the erratic motion made it nearly impossible. After several frantic attempts he managed to latch onto the handle and pull. His seat exploded and his parachute deployed. Relieved, he looked on as his plane fell from the sky, the dogfight continuing all around him. For the first time in years he said a prayer of thanks as he floated gently to the earth.

But his relief was short-lived. As he neared the ground he realized he was landing in a field next to the enemy. He hit the ground with a thud and was immediately surrounded and outnumbered by angry villagers. They attacked, stripping him down and carrying him off to a Prisoner of War compound. Life as he knew it would never be the same.

For seven years he endured unimaginable starvation, barbaric torture and worst of all— solitary confinement. He didn't know when or even if his misery was going to end. Did anyone even see him eject? Did his family know he was still alive? Would his nation come to get him? It all seemed so hopeless. But in this dark season of the soul Howard discovered the source of light.

"The sights and sounds and smells of death were all around me. My hunger for spiritual food soon outdid my hunger for a steak...I had completely neglected the spiritual dimension of my life. It took prison to show me how empty life is without God, and so I had to go back in my memory to those Sunday-school days in Tulsa, Oklahoma."

This hunger was not just his own. In the brief seconds that prisoners passed each other between cells they would quickly exchange verses of Scripture or parts of hymns. Together the prisoners formed what they would call a "living Bible."

"How I struggled to recall those Scriptures and hymns! I had spent my first eighteen years in a Southern Baptist Sunday school, and I was amazed at how much I could recall. Regrettably, I had not seen then the importance of memorizing verses from the Bible, or learning gospel songs. Now, when I needed them, it was too late. I never dreamed that I would spend almost seven years (five of them in solitary confinement) in a prison...or that thinking about one memorized verse could have made the whole day bearable.

One portion of a verse I did remember was, 'Thy word have I hid in my heart.' How often I wished I had really worked hard to hide God's Word in my heart... Remember, we weren't playing games. The enemy knew that the best way to break a man's resistance was to crush his spirit in a lonely cell.... All this talk of Scripture and hymns may seem boring to some, but it was the way we conquered our enemy and overcame the power of death around us."[i]

2 The Power of the Word

Severe trials reveal to us the foundational pillars of who we are and how we live. What Howard and so many others like him have discovered is that when all is stripped away, the pillars of our own construction are weak and tottering. Yet the joyous subsequent finding is that knowing, obeying and loving the Word of God has been and still is the very action rebuilds those foundations. David, Israel's shepherd boy turned King found the same thing.

> *"He who meditates on His Word day and night will be like a tree planted by streams of water which yields its fruit in season and whose leaf does not whither. Whatever he does, prospers" (Ps 1:3).*

Jeremiah the prophet also understood this. He restates this same Psalm:

> *"Blessed is the man who trusts in the LORD, whose confidence is in him. He will be like a tree planted by the water that sends out its roots by the stream. It does not fear when heat comes; its leaves are always green. It has no worries in a year of drought and never fails to bear fruit" (Jer 17:8).*

A life rooted and established in His Word can stand up to difficult trials. Regardless of whether we're in a time like Joseph who has been trafficked and wrongly imprisoned or in a season of influence and abundance like Abraham or King Solomon. Life can flourish when our roots run deep.

The good news is that fruitfulness can take place not only on an individual basis but also on a corporate and even national level. Consider the nation of Norway, a modern mystery to many nations. A little over a hundred years ago it was one of the poorest nations in the world. At times people ate tree bark just to survive. But today in less than one hundred years it is now on the top of the UN Human Development Index. How did Norway experience such a dramatic change?

The turnaround began with an average farmer by the name of Hans Nielsen Hauge. He had a radical encounter with the Lord and saw the power of God's Word change his life. Based on his own life experience he believed that if God could change him, God could transform every sphere of society including business, art, education, healthcare, government, entertainment, family etc... From this basis he launched more than 1000 home groups and challenged people to apply the Word in their home, work and community life. It changed a nation's history.[ii]

Something similar happened to the nation of South Korea. The whole country was embroiled in a bitter war in the 1960's. At the end of the conflict it was beaten down, poor and split into two countries. But the South Koreans began to embrace the Word of God rising early in the morning to spend long hours in prayer and study of Scripture. In only one generation South Korea went from post-war poverty to the highly developed and technology powerhouse we know today.

The pillars of one's own life and even the pillars of a nation can be restored when the Word of God is absorbed and implemented. It doesn't guarantee that there will be no hardships, that circumstances will become easier, or that one will somehow become wealthy. If anything God's Word shows us that following Him is marked by challenges and persecutions. Yet when a critical mass of society are following him or when an individual gives themselves fully to the Lord, change is the result based on the fruit-filled, transforming nature of the Word of God. But this begins with getting the Word into the very souls of our being.

3 A Journey in Memorization

Paul encourages us to let the Word of Christ dwell in us richly (Col 3:16). Not just minimally but richly. Overflowing. Abundant! If we discovered a mountain that was filled with a limitless supply of gold and anything we mined was ours, would we not want to invest our time, effort and energy acquiring this wealth? How much more do we want to mine the Word of God and fill our souls with its treasures?

In centuries past memorizing the Word was not only normal but was a necessary part of life. Books, including the Scriptures were written on scrolls and in later times, parchments. These scrolls were cumbersome, time-consuming to copy and oftentimes expensive. Not everyone had access to the scrolls and writings so memorization was essential.

Paul, Peter, and Jesus invested much time memorizing the Word as we see in the way they often quoted and referenced the Law and the Prophets. If memorization was a normal part of life in the ancient world, be encouraged that it is possible for you as well. Yet in contemporary times we often approach this subject with angst and struggling as we've often been trained to memorize via rote—the pounding of data into the head via repetition.

My own journey of Bible memorization began with the knowledge of this background. I had heard the stories of Hebrew boys memorizing the first five books of the Scriptures Bible. I thought to myself, *If they could memorize large portions of Scripture, why couldn't I?* It was a learning curve to say the least.

I started with the book of Philippians because it was short. I tackled it the best I knew how, studying the words and repeating them often. At times I could barely contain my joy in what I was discovering. There was such life in memorizing His Word as I was meditating and absorbing His truth. I was loving it! I don't remember how long it took me to finish but finally I was able to meet a friend at lunch and recite the whole book of Philippians. It was a great experience and a good start. And surprisingly enough, the whole process was easier than I thought.

The problem is that the process hindered my thirst. After that time whenever I was reading through Scripture, if I came to the book of Philippians I would skip it. I was simply burned out. This was a surprise. It was *years* before I could even look at the book of Philippians again. This avoidance wasn't exactly what I was looking for but I still recognized the good fruit from the memorization process.

A little bit later I came across a booklet entitled, "How to Memorize the New Testament in Two Years." It was based on the idea that if you memorized 20 verses a day, even if you didn't have them memorized well, the very nature of reading the Word and hearing a Sunday sermon would help with recall. If every two years you went through the

New Testament you could gain more and more memory under your belt.

This booklet sent me on a path to memorize the New Testament, Psalms and Proverbs, a goal I still have today. But the problem was that I found myself being driven along by rote and by the speed to get 20 verses memorized every single day. I was memorizing the words but not taking time to dwell on the meaning. I made it to Matthew 22 before I decided to stop. I was gaining familiarity with Scriptures but losing heart due to lack of engagement.

Still persisting I found an online memorization system that guaranteed that you could memorize 'a whole book or your money back.' I thought to myself *why not give it a try?* I figured I could use this new method to memorize the Bible. So I paid the fee and delved in. Part way through the course I realized that the method that was taught could indeed help someone memorize a book, even the Bible. But the form was similar to the 'memory palace' and was based on attaching pieces of information to different objects. I tried it. It worked. But instead of the meaning of Scripture, I was focusing mentally on looking at random objects in my imagination, not the meaning of the Scriptures. It was helpful but once more, not the road I wanted to travel.

Finally the Lord brought me to a way that has had good results, didn't cause burn out and actually is more like the way memorization took place in the ancient world. It is based on coding the information into a right-brained format to plant the left-brained information into the mind. When the right side of the brain is engaged first through story, event and visual location, the left side of the brain more readily attaches the words and data. Instead of focusing on initially getting the words memorized right away, although learning the exact wording is indeed part of the process, the focus is primarily on engaging with the story. The right brain's ability to capture memory is then leveraged to later obtain the exact word, left-brained memorization.

The long-term advantage is that the Scriptures become more real and alive when you are focusing on the story and not just the words. Additionally sections of Scripture that are confusing before you grow in revelation and understanding are put in their context. Retention is also leveraged as the mind remembers story first, data and words second. You will find yourself surprised at what is possible.

There are many benefits to Scripture memorization, most of which will come through your own journey of discovery. It can be a deeply personal process. But rest assured, memorizing large parts of Scripture is within your reach. It is neither age nor education dependent. I have watched numbers of people, as young as a 10 year-old boy who memorized the gospel of Matthew in twelve weeks as well many an older person grasping on to this process and memorizing and reciting large portions. It does take work but the fruit is worth it as Jesus is worth it all.

4 Walking with the Holy Spirit

Before we jump into the steps for memorization we must know our Helper—the promised Holy Spirit. The Holy Spirit is an often overlooked and indispensible partner in this journey of memorization. Bible teacher Amy Sollars summarizes the role of the Spirit as found in Scripture.[iii]

> "The Holy Spirit wants to aid you, assist you, help you, guide you, lead you, give you revelation of Scripture, release his gifts through you, give you boldness, teach you, strengthen you, refresh you, empower you, anoint you, protect you, fellowship with you, help you pray, give you rest, give you wisdom, reveal Jesus in your life, be your friend, and comfort you."

For you to have all this heavenly help is valuable beyond our comprehension. He wants to be involved on so many different levels. We cannot leave out what God has given us for help.

First and foundationally speaking the Spirit wants to help you understand the Scriptures. When you begin to memorize and meditate on the Bible, you will discover verses that you've probably skimmed over for years and when you slow down to commit them to memory, you are put into a position that you need that understanding.

> "the Advocate, the Holy Spirit, whom the Father will send in my name, will teach you all things" (Jn 14:26)

Ask the Lord to help as He is faithful to respond with His Spirit. How He delivers is almost like Hebrews 1:1 says, "at many times and in various ways." In my own experience, there are times when the Spirit will drop the understanding into my heart and what was confusing is suddenly made clear. At other times I will hear a sermon message or find myself reading a book that explains the very thing I prayed to understand. Trust Him to help bring you understanding.

On occasion we may think we actually know what a verse means but as we pray and ask God for greater revelation, He reveals greater understanding. For example the disciples thought they knew the Scripture but after Jesus died, he had to explain it to them again.

> "He said, "This is what I told you while I was still with you: Everything must be fulfilled that is written about me in the Law of Moses, the Prophets and the Psalms"
>
> Then he opened their minds so they could understand the Scriptures."" (Lk 24:44-45)

Another way that that the Holy Spirit comes to partner with you is through helping you to remember. It's not a remembering in the sense that He will give you the word-by-word recall (although at times He may help in that way too), but more that He reminds you of the truth found in His Word. John 14:26 says it best:

> *"...the Advocate, the Holy Spirit... will remind you of everything I have said to you."*

It's not just about whether we have a good memory or not. It's about leaning into the Holy Spirit for him to bring back those transformative truths to us.

Lastly and most importantly is that the Holy Spirit will help you to obey. It is not enough to memorize and understand but we must take action on what we know. Action with the Holy Spirit's involvement leads to transformation.

With this in mind the role of prayer cannot be undervalued in the process of memorization. Seek His assistance and for the Holy Spirit to give you greater revelation. Ask Him to show you how He wants you to obey. God is for you in this process and He longs to see you transformed more and more into His likeness. Find the power available through His partnership. It's one of the most obvious steps that we are quickest to skip. Having laid the foundations, we can now move on to the nuts and bolts.

5 The Filmmaking Memorization Process

If I asked you what you did today prior to reading this, I'm guessing with a little effort you could tell me approximately what time you woke up, what you had for breakfast, where you sat down to eat and what you did afterwards. The same is true if you go to a new restaurant in a new location and want to return. The next time you go back you typically will be able to find the restaurant more quickly by recognizing familiar landmarks from your previous visit. And you could do both these tasks of reciting what you had for breakfast and how to get to the new restaurant without any intentional effort to memorize. How is this possible?

It is because the primary form that information is stored in your mind is through <u>story, event and visual location</u>. This is the reason why you can remember what you did and where you've been. These things you don't have to consciously work to remember. They are right-brain experiences that have made impressions on your mind.

I remember once on my way to see a movie, I asked some of my friends who had watched the film the previous night to give me a small synopsis. By the time they were finished, they had given me every major plot point, character description and more. Without even trying, they had memorized almost the entire flow of the movie. After watching the movie I realized they had left nothing out.

Memory is also enhanced by the meaning and significance it holds for you personally. There was a young man I knew in college and during the first week of his sophomore year, he dreamily told everyone multiple times a day that he had "met Elaine" that day. A few minutes later he would absent-mindedly mention again that he "met a girl named Elaine." He probably couldn't remember the name of any other person he met that day but he remembered her. The following year they were married.

Whether it is a young man who has just met a beautiful woman or if it is the amount of money your new job will pay, if the information has personal significance to you, more than likely you will remember the details with little effort. When the right side of the brain is activated, the left-brain is positioned to absorb and retain information.

With this in mind everyone on earth is constantly memorizing every day. At one point you memorized your way home from work and where the fruit section is at in your preferred grocery store. You remember how to get to a friend's house and the name of your boss. Most of this memorizing comes without even trying.

Be encouraged. Our brain is a memorizing machine! It's not that we can't memorize, it's that we need methods to memorize that line up with the way that our brain learns—through story, event and visual location. This is the right-side aspect of our brain that acts like a door handle to open the left side of our brain which stores words. This is never more true than when it comes to approaching Scripture.

The memorization process that we will be looking at is called the "Film Making" method. It takes advantage of the brain's natural ability to memorize story, event and visual location. There are five steps involved:

1) Research the Relationships
2) See the Movie
3) Tell the Story
4) Attach the Words
5) Give it Away

It is good to note that these steps stand or fall together. This is easier said than done as it is surprising how quickly we tend to fall back into the old patterns of rote memorization. Rote memorization is what much of our modern education has been built upon so it's familiar. Information memorized by rote does have a tendency to be quickly remembered. But it also has a high propensity to be quickly forgotten. Our goal is long-term retention and meaningful engagement with the Scriptures. The filmmaking method may take a little more effort initially but with practice it becomes easier and even quicker. Trust the process.

6 Step One: Research the Relationships

Every good story has one key component—tension. And how is this achieved? Relationships. Put two human beings together and you'll have tension. Relationships are the foundation of all of life. When relationships are good, life is good. When relationships are being challenged, that's what makes a good story.

Every part of Scripture that you memorize is rich with relationship. Understanding these relationships will shed light on the meaning of what is being told. This is the essence of Step One—discovering and researching the relationships to establish the background. It is doing textual analysis but doing so through the lens of relationship.

There are many factors that affect relationship. Where are the people from? Where are they located? What is their gender? Role? Occupation? Status? Family background? Personality? Character?

For example a person from Nazareth, a hillbilly town with a less than notable reputation is going to relate differently to someone from Jerusalem, an important political and religious city (*the question of geography*). A person of great wealth is going to relate differently to a poor person (*the question of economic status*). A priest is going to relate differently to a peasant (*the question of social status*). A middle-eastern man is going to relate differently to a Middle-Eastern woman (*the question of gender*). An older Middle-Eastern brother is going to relate differently to his younger brother (*the question of age*). All of these factors paint the picture of what is going on in the background of relationships.

This is quite natural in everything we do. For example when we meet a new person, after getting their name the first thing we do is find out what they do for a living. How many children they have. Where they are from. It gives us context to who they are. It is the same with Scriptures. It's just that we have to ask the questions and get the answers through research.

We begin by asking how does geography, economy, social standing, family role, history, etc... play into the relationships that make this narrative? Do the individuals have good character or bad? What is the tone with which they speak to one another? Where are the tension points? What was the look on Jesus' face when He saw something happen and what was the look on the face of others when they heard Jesus?

Relationships are everything in a story. This can be done through observation, Bible-background books, maps, commentaries, Internet searches, etc. The goal is to understand these relationships through the context of the time they were written. Understanding gives us perspective.

For example in Middle-Eastern culture then and now, it is the older brother's highest responsibility to defend the honor of the family, especially the father's honor. In the Parable of the Prodigal Son when the younger brother asked the father for his inheritance while his father was still alive, it was an unspeakable insult. But culturally it fell to the oldest son/oldest brother to speak with his younger brother and bring discipline, defending the family name and the father's honor. When the older brother took his portion of the inheritance and did not bring firm correction to his younger brother, the story has shock value to a Middle Easterner. The older brother was a wicked and greedy son. It was as scandalous as the younger son's request. Tell this story in the Middle East and they will be outraged at the audacity of both sons, but with the most anger directed towards the older brother.

The context just previous to this parable is one of the Pharisees and Teachers of the Law muttering about Jesus welcoming sinners. When Jesus knew of their grumbling, he told them the story of the two sons. It looked like the parable about was the lost son, but the twist is that it was also about "the older brother" (the Pharisees) who didn't care, didn't repent and didn't honor their father's joy. Jesus was confronting them indirectly and they knew it. It was one of the reasons after he spoke this parable they wanted to kill him.

Another example of relational research affecting the storyline is found in the life of Abraham. Abraham is a person in the Bible that most people know. The average believer knows his story but do you know of his history? Do you know the name "Terah?" - the name we perhaps all should have known?

If you ask the question of relationship you will discover that when Abraham was still in Ur (modern day Iraq) with his family he had a brother that died named Haran. It was after this time that Abraham's father, Terah, received an inclination (perhaps a call?) to go to the land of Canaan. It was Terah who took his wife, his son Abraham and Abraham's wife, and his grandson Lot who was Haran's boy and set out for Canaan. One of Terah's sons strangely did not join them.

But Terah led his family north up and around the Jordan but about halfway to Canaan, he stopped. Terah had intended to go all the way to Canaan but ended at the half way point. The place where his journey ended was later named Haran, the name of Terah's son that had died. Perhaps he couldn't deal with his grief anymore. We really don't know, but for whatever reason, he stopped half way. It was a mission unfulfilled. The epitaph of Terah's journey reads, "They settled there" (Gen 11:21-32).

But God's promises and purposes were not to be foiled. The call of God was upon Abraham so he rose to the occasion. Years later he would take his wife, children and flocks and finish the journey to Canaan. But unfortunately Abraham had learned the lessons from his father about going only half way. Abraham had many problems as he told half-truths about his wife. It took him learning the hard way, almost sacrificing his son Isaac on the altar before he began to walk in full obedience to the Lord. But he did learn and through God's patience, he became the mighty patriarch that we know and love.

This is an example of how relationships develop our understanding of the story. Through relational research we see the greater context of what is happening.

While we cannot always recreate the drama of the moments of Scripture, what we can do is cultivate a deeper connection through investigating these contexts. This relational research helps us begin to lay the foundation of the text.

How much time should you spend on this step? Actually it is a process that has no ending. As you learn, study, research and gain more revelation, comprehension of the events will continue to grow. But in the beginning as you learn this process, spend enough time that you feel like you have a reasonable understanding of the text. The more you understand, the better you will memorize.

7 Step Two: See the Movie

Next time you are having coffee with a friend and you are relaying to them a story that happened to you, take note of the internal process. You will find that as you are telling the story, your mind is re-creating the event in your imagination. Your words are actually just the overflow of what you are seeing in your mind's memory.

The same is true when they tell you a story. While they are talking your mind creates a visual picture of the events that happened. When there is a gap in the picture in your mind, that's when you are likely to ask questions. "What did he do again?" "What did she say?" "How did he react to that?"

Words may change in how you tell a story but the images you've created in your mind stay the same. Your mind records stories and pictures of how you felt and experienced an event.

The problem when we practice contemporary forms of memorization is that what we tend to "see" is mainly words, not story. The visual side of our mind is dulled and a significant component of memorization is sidelined. It is possible to memorize without story but it does not do a good job making the strength of impact helpful for long-term retention. Add to this the fact that the development of the story stops as soon as the words are memorized via rote. It's why someone can burn out on memorizing a particular book.

But it brings us to a question. If we weren't there to experience the event we read about in Scripture, how do we create the visual imprints on our minds that are necessary for memorization? This is where we move to the next step which is to take the details from Step 1: Researching the Relationships, and to use those details to begin to create a filmstrip in our mind. To do this we imagine what things looked like, how people were dressed, where they are positioned in the story, what people said, etc. In essence we're re-creating what happened.

For example, take the story of the man who was healed of leprosy:

"While Jesus was in one of the towns, a man came along who was covered with leprosy. When he saw Jesus, he fell with his face to the ground and begged him, "Lord, if you are willing, you can make me clean." Jesus reached out his hand and touched the man. "I am willing," he said. "Be clean!" And immediately the leprosy left him" (Luke 5:12-16).

Here are a few of the relational details from research:

- Jesus was previously teaching by the Lake of Genessaret so he was probably in the Galilee region when he mentions "one of the towns." Galilee was not necessarily a religious center and was probably comprised more of "back country" villages of the time.

- Leprosy required that those who had it to shout loudly "Unclean!" so no one would get near. People were terrified of getting leprosy.

- For Jesus to reach out and touch the leper made Jesus ceremonially unclean but also put him at great risk to contract this disease himself.

In your mind take every detail of the story and fill it in with the information you have read and that which has been discovered. Create the story in your mind.

"While Jesus was in one of the towns"—What does this look like for you? Do you picture him being in a big city or a small village? Are there crowds around or just a few people milling about? Where was he in town? At the market or near someone's house? Pick a place.

"A man came along who was covered with leprosy"—How was the leper dressed? What did his sores look like? Did he run toward Jesus with confidence or fear? Did he look at Jesus in the eye or fall to his face? What is the reaction of the disciples? What is the reaction of the religious leaders? Are they even on the scene?

"When he saw Jesus, he fell with his face to the ground and begged him, 'Lord, if you are willing, you can make me clean.' What did this moment look like? Was he bowing down or lying on the ground prostrate? Was he crying or sobbing as he said these things? What did his begging sound like?

"Jesus reached out his hand and touched the man." What was the look on the face from the people watching when Jesus touched the unclean leper? Did anyone say anything? What was the look in Jesus' eyes? What was the look in the leper's eyes?

"I am willing," he said. "Be clean!" And immediately the leprosy left him." What was the look on the leper's face when Jesus said he was willing? Was he shocked? Did the leper begin examining his arms and legs to see if it was true or did he instantly believe his words? What did he say? What did he do? How did the crowd react? What did the disciples do?

In this step you look at all the details and begin asking yourself, 'if I were to make a movie out of this scene, what would it look like?' Where would they be standing and how would they be speaking to each other?

Now that you have the picture in your mind, slowly go through the text again and "see" the movie unfold in your imagination. Re-read the text making sure you get all the parts of the story. The sharper the details and images the better you will be able to remember the story.

This perhaps is the most key aspect of this process. If you get the story pictured firmly in your mind, memorization will come much easier. And the nice thing about capturing the story is that it never ends; it can continue to develop as you grow in understanding of the events. The more you study and get revelation, the richer the picture develops.

It is good to note that during this time you are not yet attaching the exact words. The focus of Step 2 is to create as clear a picture as possible in your mind.

8 Hide and Seek

Getting the story is foundational as story is what will imprint the text on your mind and make the text meaningful and memorable. This allows for easier attachment of the exact words. But the different genres of Scripture lend themselves to different levels of storyline. Sometimes we get a narrative text that has rich detail. Stories like the life of Joseph are highly descriptive. In fact a large portion of the Bible is straightforward storytelling. But what do you do when you're trying to research the relationships yet the story isn't obvious?

We often find this in places like the Psalms where sometimes we don't have any background information as to why it was written, not even the clue "of David." But just because we don't know the background outright doesn't mean there's not a context to place it into.

Consider an example from a diary entry from one of my family members. What would you be able to discern about the back-story of this occasion with just a simple statement?

"Today the radio was blaring news of war."

1) Which war do you think this might be?

    a) Civil War
    b) WW I
    c) WW II
    d) Operation: Desert Storm

2) Approximately when do you think she would have written this?

    a) 1812
    b) 1915
    c) 1944
    d) 1991

In the first question we can rule out the Civil War and WW I because radio wasn't a primary means of communication for the general public during those time periods; Communication was mainly through newspapers. Both WW II and the Iraqi war are both viable options because radio was around, but we would probably be more likely to infer WW II as radio was the prevailing form of communication. After the proliferation of TV and Internet, radio fell away as a primary means of news broadcast. Therefore if we can presume the first question is WW II, then the second question would naturally be an entry written in 1944 based on the options given. This is how we look at details to discover background. We use this same type of process when looking at Scripture. We look at the clues to determine the story.

But what if you have virtually nothing to go on and very few clues? This is where you look at what is written and make inferences as to what could be going on behind the scenes. Perhaps a Psalm is crying out for God's protection. You could assume that a foreign enemy was attacking the psalmist in some way. You could then look at the times in David's life when he was at war and choose one of those situations. Perhaps it is a psalm of praise and worship. You could infer that it might be a temple song or a response to something good God has done. You work to find a plausible event that this scenario could be placed into based on the clues and then choose an event.

If you are unable to find a likely scenario and have run out of possible incidents in which to connect the story, then place the Scripture into a relevant story from your own life. Perhaps a psalm of suffering could be placed into a time in your life where you have suffered. Or a time of jubilant praise could be placed into the story of a season of great joy in your life.

Why is it so important to find the story in the background? Because every text needs a context to build a story and story is an important key for long-term retention.

If you're the kind who needs something tangible in front of you for visual purposes, cut and paste pictures into a document or even draw a picture. You can even make a video of still images. Strong visual connection to the text is going to help you imprint the text on your mind and again, make it memorable.

9 Location, Location, Location

Story and event are powerful for memorization and seeing the story (Step Two), but the other component is visual location. Where you see the story unfolding as well as the choreography of those within the story help bring understanding to the text. This is part of how you "watch" the story in your mind unfold.

First of all we need to have an idea of the geographic location of the events. It doesn't mean you need precise details and borders but rather the general idea of the location.

For example, if you're memorizing the Gospels and it mentions Jesus was preaching in Galilee, picture Israel and the region of Galilee. If you use a Bible map you will discover that Galilee is in the northern part of Israel with its big lake. If it says Judea, then your image should be in the south of Israel, which is mostly although not exclusively arid desert. If the verse talks about Jerusalem, then know that Jerusalem is just west of the tip of the Dead Sea. Again you don't need to memorize the whole map but rather have an idea of the location so you can place it in your mind. The best way to do this is to actually draw a map on a piece of paper with the relevant locations.

Location though is more than just geography of the land. Like any movie that is made, it is important to know where the people are located in the story. Are the people standing nearby or far away? Where are they looking? What are their movements? Creating placement is a helpful tool

For example let's look at Psalm 4. Take a moment and read this psalm and try to picture the progression in your mind.

> *Answer me when I call to you,*
> *O my righteous God.*
> *Give me relief from my distress;*
> *be merciful to me and hear my prayer.*
>
> *How long, O men, will you turn*
> *my glory into shame?*
> *How long will you love delusions*
> *and seek false gods?*
> *Know that the LORD has set*
> *apart the godly for himself;*
> *the LORD will hear when I call to him.*
>
> *In your anger do not sin;*
> *when you are on your beds,*
> *search your hearts and be silent.*
> *Offer right sacrifices and trust in the LORD.*
> *Many are asking,*
> *'Who can show us any good?'*
> *Let the light of your face shine upon us,*
> *O LORD.*
>
> *You have filled my heart with*
> *greater joy than when their grain*
> *and new wine abound.*
> *I will lie down and sleep in peace,*
> *for you alone, O LORD,*
> *make me dwell in safety.*

Initially the psalm may seem challenging as it shifts from a prayer to God (v. 1), then jumps to talking about outsiders (v. 2-3), next addressing worshipers or perhaps his military cabinet (v. 4-6), and then back to speaking with the Lord (v. 7-8). The cohesion could be difficult to track but with location helps the progression can be made more clear and memorable.

Let's look at this Psalm establishing location points. In the prelude of the Psalm we read that it is "of David" so that helps set the authorship. But we have no specific mention that tells us the context. This is where we need to create a back-story as best as we can. To do this we examine the psalm and discern as much about the background as possible.

We know that David had enemies who were defiling the name of the Lord. We know that he is also addressing people who are seeking the ways of God. Perhaps David is fleeing from Saul and is in the cave as this was an event where he was confronting his enemies. Maybe David is in his palace and things are getting tense right before his own son, Absalom, overthrows him. We don't know for sure but this is where we choose a plausible context.

Let's connect this psalm to the conflict with his son Absalom who was trying to overthrow his father's kingdom.

<u>Location Point 1</u>. Imagine David in his palace and he's on the second floor. Outside are those who hate him and want to overthrow his reign. They are angry and protesting. His own son has swayed their hearts against him and he is deeply grieved. His fellow God-fearers and his advisors are in the room with him. He is in front on them all with his back turned away and his head covered as he quietly prays to the Lord: *"Answer me when I call to you, O my righteous God. Give me relief from my distress; be merciful to me and hear my prayer."*

Location Point 2. At this point picture him wandering over to the window and looking down into the street only to see men who are angry and throwing objects at the palace. They are also holding up idols in their hands as they make a mockery of the One True God. As David is looking out the window, half praying and half pleading, he says quietly to himself, *"How long, O men, will you turn my glory into shame? How long will you love delusions and seek false gods? Know that the LORD has set apart the godly for himself; the Lord will hear when I call to him."*

Location Point 3. Next imagine him turning to the people in the room. They are his military cabinet, friends and advisors who are known to be righteous. He faces them even as he points out the window. He addresses his fellow God-fearers in the room as they are angry and muttering against this wickedness. They may even be plotting how to kill the rebels. He addresses them pastorally saying, *"In your anger do not sin; when you are on your beds, search your hearts and be silent. Offer right sacrifices and trust in the LORD."* Many are asking, *"Who can show us any good?" Let the light of your face shine upon us, O LORD."*

Back to Location Point 1. Now picture David turning away from them again in prayer with eyes lifted toward heaven. *"You have filled my heart with greater joy than when their grain and new wine abound,"* he says, pointing out the window when he says "their." *"I will lie down and sleep in peace, for you alone, O LORD, make me dwell in safety."*

Take a moment and reread the psalm in its entirety with these location points in mind. Does it make the psalm more clear and memorable?

What we did was take an event that may or may not have happened in David's life and with the details given created a storyline. Perhaps you imagine another event in David's life. The story in one person's mind may be different than someone else's and that is okay as long as we are staying true to the text. But find a story that fits the context as best as possible and create the filmstrip in your imagination. Keep in mind the location when creating your story, both the geographic location as well as the positioning of the people involved.

10 Step Three: Tell the Story

The first step was to look at the story through the lens of relationship to understand the factors that affect the story. The second step was to create a movie in your mind as if you were an eyewitness of these events. Now we go to the third step and that is paraphrase.

When you come to the point of paraphrase, you want to be able to tell every detail of the story but to do so in your own words (and without looking at the text). This strengthens the images in your mind and the story progression. It also demonstrates your understanding of the text and the details within it.

We're still not to the stage of attaching the exact words so use your own words at this point. Tell this story as if you were there and it is an eyewitness account. If you have not created a strong story with a high sense of details in the first two steps, you will be limited when you try to put it into your own words. If you've done Step 1 and Step 2 well, this should be a fairly easy step.

Here's an example of a paraphrase that could've been made from the healing of the leper:

"Jesus was walking through one of the towns when a man came up who had leprosy from head to toe. It was nasty. When the man saw Jesus, instead of calling out "unclean!" he went to him and begged him

for healing. He kept saying, "Lord, if you're willing you can make me clean." The disciples and the religious leaders were beside themselves.

Then Jesus did the unthinkable. He reached out his hand and touched the man. You heard me right, he touched him! Then he told him, "I am willing, be clean!" And would you believe it?! That guy was healed! There was not a spot of leprosy on him ANYWHERE!"

Everyone's paraphrase will look and sound different as we are all different. This is good as it needs to be in your own words and sound like you telling it. But it also needs to resemble the story of the text as much as possible and be reflective of your research.

A key element is that you need to speak this <u>out loud</u>. This may mean telling your pillow or the cat or dog. Ideally it is best to sit down with someone over coffee and tell him or her about this event you "saw." The biggest factor is to not let this be in your head alone. Everything changes when you begin to speak it out.

So why paraphrase? This is to continue to solidify not only all the details of the story but to make sure that the storyline is fully embedded in your imagination. If the details aren't clear in your mind, this is where you will stumble when attaching the words. When you can say it out loud using your own words, hitting all the main details and seeing the picture in your mind, you are ready to move on to the next step.

11 Step Four: Attach the Words

Your work with the first three steps will form the foundation for attaching the exact and actual words. If you've done the previous steps well, this will become easier although it will still take time.

To begin with have your text in front of you in a small chunk (around 6-10 verses). Look at the words and pick the first short phrase which should be approximately 3-5 words. Remembering the movie of that incident, visualize that part of the scene in your mind and attach those 3-5 words.

For example in the story of the healing of the leper, look down and read the words, "While Jesus was in one of the towns." Remember your "film-strip" of a village town with villagers scattered about. See it in your imagination. While you work on remembering the picture you've created in your mind, attach the words by saying them out loud—"While Jesus was in one of the towns." Do this several times if necessary to match the words to the picture in your mind.

Next look at the phrase "a man came along who was covered with leprosy." Look at the movie in your mind of Jesus walking through town, and then a man comes along covered with leprosy. Then say the words, "While Jesus was going through one of the towns, a man came along who was covered with leprosy."

At this point you can continue in one of two ways. You can continue to embed each additional phrase into your memory going through the whole section of 6-10 verses. Or you can add a phrase, review from the beginning, add another phrase, review from the beginning again, etc... The key point is "seeing" the picture in your mind's eye while the words of the text are attaching to the story. It's important to not attach the picture to the words but the words to the picture.

One caution is that if you find yourself struggling to remember the exact words, stop what you're doing and take time to look at the text. It's better that you see the words rather than to strive to remember the words disconnected to the picture.

Keep the filmstrip in your head as much as possible while attaching the words. Soon you will find that the exact words will start to attach to the story. It does take practice so don't expect perfection from the beginning. This is a learned skill that once learned, can accelerate the memorization process. And be sure to do as much of this as possible out loud. Why?

12 Out Loud

In 383 AD Augustine, the first emperor of the Christian world remarked with amazement at his mother's advisor Ambrose. "When he reads," said Augustine, "his eyes scanned the page and his heart sought out the meaning, but his voice was silent and his tongue was still!"[iv]

Silent reading as is done today was a remarkable and curious endeavor. Ancient libraries were not the places of silence but rather a cacophony of readers. Do you remember Philip in Acts 8? He was walking along the road when he came across the Ethiopian Eunuch in his chariot reading out loud from the book of Isaiah. He was reading out loud not because he was on a deserted road and no one would hear him but because this was the normative way to read.

The result of reading out loud is that the mind engages, the mouth speaks and the ears hear, an effective tool for memory. In similar practice, it is good also to practice the Scriptures out loud. There are two reasons for doing so.

The first is that speaking the Scriptures out loud greatly enhances your ability to remember when your ears hear what the mouth speaks. So often we meditate on the Word and memorize it but it stays in the recesses of our mind. What you will discover is that when you review the Scriptures to yourself, you are nothing short of brilliant in recall. But when you begin to speak it out loud, especially to someone else, your previous pat-yourself-on-the-back recall vanishes like the morning mist.

The second reason is that speaking the Scriptures out loud helps you to practice using Scripture for ministry moments. Opportunities to share the Word of God often arise and when they do, we want to be confident in being able to share the Word to someone else. We will look at this more in the next chapter.

13 Step Five: Give it Away

Scripture memorization is not for self-edification alone. The Word of Christ in its happiest form flows through you for the blessing of others. You will find that when you discover how it can benefit others, it will inspire you to memorize even more.

Having said this, it doesn't mean that we load our Scripture guns and shoot out verses at everyone who comes our way. How we use Scripture in conversation, the context and the spirit with which we engage Scripture with others matters tremendously. We want to use the Word graciously and with wisdom so that it can encourage and build up one other. It may even start them on their own process of Scripture discovery.

Imparting the Word and getting it outside of ourselves has many and various forms. Here are a few suggestions:

1) **Write down your discoveries.** Whether you do this for outreach such as in a blog or for your own personal journaling, this is very helpful. You don't want to lose what the Lord reveals to you. The more you begin to memorize and delve into his Word the more He will reveal Himself to you. "Draw near to me and I will draw near to you," the Lord says. And if you choose to use a blog, you never know when your discovery or something you write blesses someone else.

Additionally there are times when you will reread your journal entries only to be surprised at some of the discoveries that you've recorded and have already forgotten. Keeping them logged is a wonderful way to hold on to those discoveries. So whether it is for yourself and/or to share with the world, write down what you've found and learned.

2) Share Scripture portions with friends. One way that you can Scripture with others is when you're on a road trip or having breakfast with friends or family. Let them know you've been working on a section of Scripture and would it be Ok if you could recite it to them. This is good practice as it often leads to great discussion of the Scriptures. It becomes a time of mutual edification.

3) Use Scripture stories for evangelism. Imagine choosing the longest line in a super-market and asking to share a Scripture story with the person standing with you in line. A 30-second Scripture story may be the very seed of truth that they need to hear. You don't always need to preach afterwards (unless the Lord leads you), but Jesus often ministered to people with a story. Or how about the next time you are sitting in a doctor's office you share with the person next to you? Stories are powerful tools for evangelism.

4) Gospel presentations. This is an effective way for people to hear the story from Scripture and as people who have memorized the Word present it in dramatic form. Listeners connect with Scripture differently when they hear it spoken.

5) Teach others. Sometimes you learn something the best when you are put in the position to teach it. Gather a small group of friends together or teach a class at your church.

Ask God to use the Scripture He has placed in you for the edification of others. He will surprise you with how he will use you to minister to others. And that's our goal, that memorization would not just be for our edification alone but for the pleasure of the Lord and to strengthen His people.

14 Forget It!

Forgetfulness is not typically a good thing but when it comes to the memorization process it is actually an essential part of retention. If you were taking a foreign language and had the option of a taking a one-month intensive course all day long every day, or taking that same course spread out over four months, which would you take? You might be able to pass the test after taking the first course but to embed the information in your long-term memory, you would do better to take the second option. The brain needs intervals of rest or times of "forgetting" for optimal retention.

This science was researched primarily in the 1885 by Ebbinghaus and was called the "forgetting curve."[v] Ebbinghaus logged his ability to remember non-sensical information and graphed his retention or lack thereof. Later researchers would build on the understanding of the forgetting curve and try to determine at what intervals of rest between material were needed for optimal retention. This research is called by a number of different names such as "spaced repetition" or the "spacing effect."

What this looks like in the process of Scripture memorization is that you need to have a strong initial understanding and memorization of the material, but then give it ever increasing intervals of rest between review. In a three-month time it actually isn't ideal to recite a text every single day. Perhaps review it every day for the first two to three weeks. Then take a few days of rest before returning to it again. Then taking a week break before coming back to it. And then again several more weeks before revisiting the text again. Greater and greater distance between review will actually be more helpful in the long run. It exposes the weaker points which is what we want. We need to know which areas need strengthening.

Make it a goal to have spoken a section out loud 40x, at least 15 of those times to other people in the first 3 months. You will find that the first 20 times may go smooth, but then a rough patch tends to occur in the 20-30 range which will eventually smooth out again. It is a process that can last several months. Find what works best for you but just know that time away from the text, then review, with ever increasing time away from the text is a more powerful way to reinforce what you've learned.

With the advent of smart phone technology review can also be enhanced through various apps. Use a recorder app to listen to your voice, create the story and/or check the accuracy. You can use a multiple hit counter app to keep track of how many times you've reviewed each Scripture. A Bible app on your phone can be helpful when you're sitting and waiting in line somewhere or at the doctor's office. Be creative with the tools that help you to review.

15 Memorizing Lists

Having learned all these steps, how does this apply to lists? Wouldn't we rather avoid things such as genealogies?

In the heart of Papua New Guinea some of my friends were working on a Bible translation. They came to the place that the missionaries honestly found boring—the genealogy. Up to this point the translation of portions of Scripture had been only marginally received and they wondered what effect the genealogy would have. Was it even worth their time to translate when there were so many other important texts yet to translate? They made the decision that it was part of Scripture and what they were doing so they translated the long list of names.

What they discovered was a shock. The tribe they were working with became excited and a buzz erupted among the people.

"It's true!" They said. "The Scriptures are true!"

Bewildered, the missionaries began to ask questions to figure out the reason for this joyous eruption. What they discovered was that in the culture of that particular tribe, if you had a genealogy it meant you had a heritage and therefore the story was true. The translation of the genealogy became an unexpected door opener for the reception of the rest of the Scriptures.

When it comes to memorizing lists such as genealogies, they are still Scripture and do have their place in God's epic story. In order to memorize lists such as these we take a modified approach but one that still captures visual images in our mind. This method has been used for centuries and is often referred to as the Chain Method. It connects and links different images together so you can memorize a large number of pieces of information.

It is based on the premise that the mind has an ability to firmly store two images at the same time. With each additional piece of information, the ability to hold on to those items becomes less and less, but it can handle two items well.

So what do you do when you have a list of multiple items? Let's look at 10 completely random objects that have no relationship to each other.

Refrigerator—basketball—arrow—curtain—toothbrush—mouse—microwave—cell phone—shoe—milk jug

The process works by picturing only two images in your mind at a time. See in your imagination the first image while placing the second image 1) On top, 2) To the right or 3) Piercing the first image. Then add the next image (dropping the first image from your mind) but only keeping two images in your mind at a time, placing this next image on top, to the right or piercing the previous image. Let's practice with the first five objects.

The first two objects are the refrigerator and the basketball. See the refrigerator in your mind and for our sake let's place the basketball on top of the refrigerator. Do you have it pictured? Now shift your focus and in your mind see the basketball, and let's take the arrow and imagine it piercing the basketball and sticking out to the right. So you should only be seeing the basketball with the arrow sticking out to the right. Now in your mind enlarge the arrow and have a giant curtain hanging from the shaft of the arrow. See only the arrow and the curtain. Then imagine the curtain and picture a large toothbrush piercing the curtain. In your mind see only the curtain with the toothbrush sticking out. Without looking, test it out and see if you can list the first five items beginning with the refrigerator. Now practice adding the remaining elements from the list. If you have trouble remembering, it's probably because the pictures need to be more vivid in your imagination.

Once you are able to do this successfully, let's move to the genealogy of Jesus as we read in Luke 3. Joseph is the obvious parental figure of Jesus that we see in many a nativity so usually we can remember—Jesus, son of Joseph. Now we add the rest of the names that for most of us are unfamiliar.

The way to handle this is to code the words in such a way that they can create some kind of familiar visual image in your mind. For example with Heli, you might think of the Greek word Heli which means "sun." So Joseph could be pictured holding a shining sun to the right. The next name on the list is Matthat. Picture a person named Matt that you know (familiar or famous) standing on the sun. The next name is Levi. Perhaps a way to picture this is to imagine a priest in a colorful Levitic robe putting an arm around the shoulders of the person you know called Matt. The next name is Melchi. It looks like the word "milk." So you could put a jug of milk balancing on top of the Levite's head. Each subsequent image is on top of, to the right or piercing the first image. So now you should have the names Joseph, Heli, Matthat, Levi and Melchi.

Keep only two images in your mind at a time. Look and see Joseph holding a sun, then see Matt (Matthat) standing on top of the sun, then Levi with his arm around Matt (Matthat), and then a jug of milk (Melchi) on Matt's (Matthat) head. Now take a moment to review. Once you have those down continue to add more names, taking time to review as you go along.

Genealogies aren't the only places where you will find lists. Consider the Sermon on the Mount which has approximately 20 short teachings of Jesus. It's good as you memorize the Sermon on the Mount to know these stories in order. You can approach this also using the Chain Method. Give each teaching an object that represents the text and then attach the next object on top, to the right or piercing the first object.

For example, the first five teachings are the Beatitudes, Salt of the Earth, Light of the World, Fulfillment of the Law and Adultery. If you give each section an object, it could look like the following:

Beatitudes—A Priest (for blessing)
Salt of the Earth—Saltshaker
Light of the World—A lamp
Murder—A gun
Adultery—Lipstick

Your working objects therefore are the following:

Priest—Saltshaker—Lamp—Gun—Lipstick

To begin with picture a priest with his hand out to the side. In his hand is a saltshaker. See the priest with the saltshaker in his outstretched hand. Then enlarge the saltshaker in your mind and place a large, bright lamp on top. See those two objects only, then picture the lamp with a gun piercing the lampshade.

Then picture a giant tube of lipstick stuck on the hammer of the gun. So now you have images for the first five teachings. When you connected these back to the teachings, you then remember that the order is the Beatitudes, Salt of the Earth, Light of the World, Murder and Adultery.

With some practice, you will be able to memorize not only forwards but also backwards. Give it a try.

16 How to Get Started

Now that you have the tools to start, how do you move forward? Let's review the steps:

- Step One: Research the Relationships
- Step Two: See the Movie
- Step Three: Tell the Story
- Step Four: Attach the Words
- Step Five: Give it Away

The first thing you need to do is choose a Scripture passage to memorize. A gospel story is perhaps one of the best places to begin as it is already in story form. Perhaps begin with the text we've used earlier with the leper coming to Jesus (Luke 5:12-16).

Secondly create a working document. When you are memorizing large portions of Scripture, it is helpful to put it into a word processing document, double-spaced and with the chapter titles and verse numbers removed. The reason is that originally the chapters and verses were added hundreds of years later. This has been helpful for research purposes but it can distract from the story. We at times don't even realize that stories are connected to each other as they are broken up by chapter markers. At other times stories are labeled in such a way that it distracts from the meaning. (Imagine how you would see the Parable of the Prodigal Son differently if it were labeled "Parable of the Running Father" or "Parable of the Evil Older Brother.")

Third is to <u>work the process</u>. In the first two steps of Researching the Relationships and Seeing the Movie, we have a tendency to speed through it quickly. But if we slow down and do these well, the other pieces will come together much more quickly and with much more longevity.

17 Caution Lights

Every good road has a few caution lights. This is true even with Scripture memorization. Here are a few that I've learned from experience:

1) <u>Forgetting to pray and seek the Lord</u>—It's easy to get so goal-focused that we forget to include the Lord in the process. Seek the Lord not just with your mind and heart but with your spirit and soul as well. He longs to reveal Himself through His word. This isn't just a journey of memorization but of growing relationally with the Lord and for one another.

2) <u>Putting goals above process</u>. Set your direction firmly but your time frames with grace. You don't want to become so driven that you lose the process of absorbing and digesting the Scriptures.

3) <u>Boasting/pride</u>—When you begin to tell people how many Scriptures or books of the Bible you've memorized, it may be a good sign that you're goal has superseded the ultimate goal of Jesus.

4) <u>Not taking times of rest</u>—Remember that taking a break from a section of Scripture is a part of the memory process. Another caution is that too much rest is equally not beneficial.

5) <u>Appropriate pacing</u>—Memorizing large portions is not a sprint but a marathon. When you run a sprint you

go as fast as you possible. When you run a marathon you hold yourself back so that you can run the distance. Go at the speed of developing your relationship with the Lord.

6) <u>Make sure there is review</u>—No process is perfect in keeping the Word fresh. It's the process of review that helps keep it alive.

7) <u>Falling back into habits of rote</u>—It's quicker to go back to rote as it does have short-term success. But for longer-term success, this method is very fruitful.

8) <u>Trusting the process</u>—This is a five step process (1)—Researching the relationships, 2)—See the Movie, 3)—Tell the story, 4)—Attach the words, 5)—Give it Away and for this method to work, it all stands or falls together.

9) <u>Not writing down discoveries</u>. When you don't write it down, it becomes quickly forgotten and lost.

10) <u>Thinking you don't have enough time</u>. "One of the great uses of Twitter and Facebook will be to prove at the Last Day that prayerlessness was not from lack of time," says John Piper. The same could be said of all spiritual disciplines.

18 Maximizing Memory

There are things we can do maximize memory. What we put in can often be what we get out.

1) A healthy brain is a happy brain. Just like the rest of our body our brain needs food, water and oxygen to thrive. Poor quality food, low hydration and lack of exercise reduces our ability to absorb and remember. If we want to solidify the Word of God in our hearts, it means taking care of our whole selves.

2) Life is better when we are together. Oftentimes we work best when we share the journey with others. The same is true with Scripture. When we do life in the Word together we get a lot farther along. For planners this may look like regularly held practice sessions. For spontaneous folks, it means calling up your friends when you want to recite Scripture or going to them when you need to practice. Also when we look at Scripture to research the relationships, there is such richness in exploring the Scripture with your brothers and sisters in Christ, especially those from different cultures and/or socio-economic backgrounds.

3) The more you give the more you get. The more you pray and discover ways to give away the Word that is now treasured in your heart, the more you will be encouraged to dive more deeply into the Word. Pray and seek ways to serve others with the Word you are learning.

4) Obedience is God's Love Language. We treasure His Word in our hearts so that the lives we live will bring His joy. This is the whole focus of memorizing His Word, that we love Him in the way that brings joy to His heart.

19 A Woman at War

It was as if the Lord had prepared her many years before. Darlene Diebler was a missionary in the jungles of New Guinea. She was actually one of the first European woman to follow her husband into the Baliem Valley to bring the gospel of Jesus to an area known for cannibalism. She had braced herself for these hardships, but there was one she hadn't prepared for. In September of 1945 there was a foreign invasion that overtook New Guinea. Darlene, her husband and her colleagues were carried off to a Prison of War camp.

They tried to take everything from them. The separated the men from the woman, gave them limited rations of food, and tried to bury their faith. It was a difficult season of the soul, and yet there was light.

> *"As a child and young person, I had had a driving compulsion to memorize the written Word. In the cell I was grateful now for those days in Vacation Bible School, when I had memorized many single verses, complete chapters, as well as whole books of the Bible.*
>
> *In the years that followed, I reviewed the Scriptures often. The Lord fed me with the Living Bread that had been stored against the day when fresh supply was cut off by the loss of my Bible. He brought daily comfort and encouragement—yes, and*

> *joy—to my heart through the knowledge of the Word."*
>
> "Paul, the apostle, wrote that it was through the comfort of the Scriptures that he had hope and steadfastness of heart to believe God. I had never needed the Scriptures more than in these months on death row, but since so much of His Word was there in my heart, it was not the punishment anticipated when they took my Bible."[vi]

Darlene would write these words even after she lost her husband to starvation and disease. We never know how the Word planted in us will be used by the Lord. But we do know that His Word will not return void.

Author Notes

It is my hope that this writing has spurred you on to engage in Scripture memorization. You will discover that memorizing the Scripture is like a tree that continually bears fruit in season. The key is to not give up and to pace yourself. Make it a marathon and not the sprint. Enjoy the process. May the Lord bless you and keep you as you engage in your journey with Him.

Questions, need help, comments or testimonies?

Would you like a seminar at your church?

ohanaofheaven@gmail.com

For author's blog of Scripture discoveries:

http://memorizationandmeditation.blogspot.com

If this book has been helpful to you, please consider leaving a review on Amazon. Your words matter to other potential readers more than even the author's description. My goal by making this at the lowest price possible is to reach the most number of people possible.

Appendix A:
Practice with Luke 17:11-19

"Now on his way to Jerusalem, Jesus traveled along the border between Samaria and Galilee. As he was going into a village, ten men who had leprosy met him. They stood at a distance and called out in a loud voice, "Jesus, Master, have pity on us!"

When he saw them, he said, "Go, show yourselves to the priests." And as he went, they were cleansed.

One of them, when he saw he was healed, came back, praising God in a loud voice. He threw himself at Jesus' feet and thanked him—and he was a Samaritan.

Jesus asked, "Were not all ten cleansed? Where are the other nine? Was no one found to return and give praise to God except this foreigner?" Then he said to him, "Rise and go; your faith has made you well."

Step 1: Research the Relationships

This is a map of Israel. Research and label the locations that are mentioned in the text.

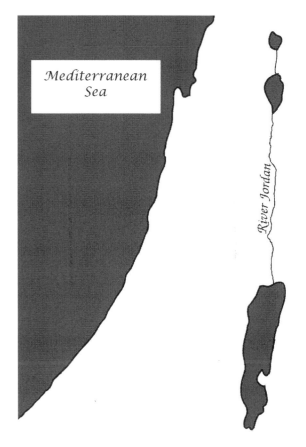

Questions for Research

1. How does this story relate to the bigger picture?

2. What is going on behind scenes?
   a) What is going on in the context of the book itself?
   b) How does it fit into what the author of the book is saying in the bigger picture?
   c) What in the historical context is important?

3. What is the geographic development?
   a) What do we know about these areas?
   b) Is there any historical significance to these cities/areas that are important?

4. What role do the following play in relationships? And how?

   a) Economic status/job/position
   b) Family role
   c) Age
   d) Gender
   e) Ethnicity
   f) Political environment
   g) Religious environment
   h) Time (hour, day, season, year)

5. Who are the people involved? How do they relate to the others? What is the tone of voice in their interaction? What is their character? How was Jesus seeing them?

Notes:

Example: The general Jewish population hated the Samaritans and would typically cross the Jordan River to the other side to avoid Samaria. The borders perhaps were places of tension.

Step 2: See the Movie

Read each phrase of the text and in your mind picture the details. For example,
"Now on his way to Jerusalem"—We know Jesus was traveling south because he was in the northern region. Was he with his disciples? Was he alone?

"Jesus traveled along the border between Samaria and Galilee." Picture the border and the location.

"As he was going into a village." Did the village have walls or a tower? What did the houses look like? Were there a lot of people or just a few? Was this a Jewish village or a Samaritan village?

"ten men who had leprosy met him." They wouldn't have been allowed to enter the city. So how did they get close enough to see Jesus as he was entering? Had they heard he was coming? Were they anticipating his arrival? What did they look like?

"They stood at a distance." How far away did they stand? In your mind as he is entering the town, are they off to the right or to the left?

Step 3: Tell the Story

Get a friend or your pillow, your cat, your dog or anything and tell them this story. Try to do so seeing the picture of the event in your mind and getting all the detail

Step 4: Add the Words

- Picture Jesus heading south towards Jerusalem. Then say the words, "Now on his way to Jerusalem." Make sure you first have the picture in your mind prior to embedding the words.

- Now determine the location of the border between Samaria and Galilee. Start with you image of Jesus on his way to Jerusalem and add the next part: "Now on his way to Jerusalem, Jesus traveled along the border between Samaria and Galilee.

- Picture Jesus going into the village and add this phrase. So you have, "Now on his way to Jerusalem, Jesus traveled along the border between Samaria and Galilee. As he was going into a village,"

- Continue with the rest of the phrases making sure you first see the picture in your mind, then add the words. If you find yourself struggling to remember the words, pause to look at them on your paper.

Step 5: Give it Away
Find a way to share with others. Here are some suggestions:

1) Blogging/Journal

2) Sharing with your family at breakfast.

3) Sharing with a co-worker.

4) Do a one-minute presentation in your church.

5) Teach someone how to memorize the text.

Works Cited

[i] Rutledge, Howard. *In the Presence of Mine Enemies.* Flemming Revell Company: Old Tappan, NJ 1973, pgs 34-37.

[ii] Cunningham, Loren and Rogers, Janice. *The Book that Transforms Nations.* Seattle, WA: YWAM Publishing, 2007. Pgs 65-71.

[iii] Amy Sollars, www.amysollars.com. PDF file: "The Holy Spirit."

[iv] Alberto Manguel, Chapter 2 of *A History of Reading* (New York; Viking, 1996).

[v] http://psychology.about.com/od/cognitivepsychology/p/forgetting.htm

[vi] Pg. 143. *Evidence not seen: A woman's miraculous faith in a Japanese prison camp during WWII/* by Darlene Diebler/Rose. San Francisco, CA Harer and Row 1941.

Made in the USA
Coppell, TX
31 October 2022

85509239R00042